the minimalist budget

SAVE MONEY, SPEND LESS, LIVE MORE

by steve h. willis

table of contents

introduction

The word "budget" has a lot of negative connotations, and it all has to do with the fact that we always feel as though it implies that we will be deprived of certain comforts if we chose to create and stick to one. Budgeting isn't as difficult a concept as we make it out to be, but most of us tend to dread it because it feels as though we are imposing limitations on ourselves—and that makes us dislike the general idea of it. When it comes to the technical aspects of budgeting, the only math that is involved in the process is fully understood by prepubescent children. Hence, if you really think about it, our difficulties with budgeting aren't based on us lacking the technical skills to do it—they are based on our mindsets and our general attitudes towards the subject.

We are afraid of budgeting because it means that we have to give up some of the material things that we enjoy so much—but what if we could change our mindsets and begin to see that those material possessions aren't that important, after all? What if we told you that you are better off attaching value to great personal experiences instead of material things?

Minimalism is a lifestyle choice that is based on the core belief that material possessions are unimportant and that one can attain true happiness by putting an end to the pursuit of material wealth and instead focusing on things that fill their lives with joy and passion. Originally, minimalism was an art form that was linked with aspects such as purity and intentionality—but now, it is a way of life that stands in stark contrast with consumerism.

Minimalism is the process of discovering the things that are essential to your life so that you can focus all your resources and mental energy on those things and that you can stop wasting your time and money on other things.

When you look at life from the point of view of a minimalist, your understanding of what's truly important in life changes significantly. Hence, when you think of budgeting, instead of looking at it as something that deprives you of the joys of life, you begin seeing it as a tool that can help you eliminate the wastes in your life.

When you look at the debt statistics of different generations and different countries across the world, you will be able to observe the fact that the amount of debt that certain generations and communities possess depend on their values and their view of consumerism. The youngest generation in the workforce today is Generation Z, most of whom are currently aged between 18 and 21. This generation is still young, and even some of the oldest among them are still in college. They currently have access to credit cards, and while most of them still have stellar credit scores, many of them seem to be taking up student loans at a faster rate than the generations before them.

Millennials are currently in their 20s and their early thirties. You keep hearing many stereotypical characterizations of millennials, their work ethics, and their spending habits. While most of those negative stereotypes are exaggerated, some of them are based on real evidence. For example, millennials with college degrees are forced to take up low-paying or even minimum-wage jobs because many great job opportunities are tied up by earlier generations. As a result, millennials generally underperform when it comes to paying off credit card bills and student loans. In the US, millennials who have mortgages have managed to pay off only 8% of those loans, on average, which means that millennial homeowners owe an average of about $200,000 in ongoing and future mortgage payments.

The members of Generation X are in their mid to late 30s and their 40s, with the oldest being about 50 years old in 2019. They have the highest mortgage rate of any generation, and the homeowners among them owe an average of over $230,000. They also have an additional non-mortgage debt (i.e., car payments, student loans, etc.) of over $30,000, on average. That means that the average Gen-Xer has a debt accumulating way over a quarter of a million dollars!

The baby boomers are in their 50s and 60s. Even though they have been in the workforce for several decades now and though some of them are retiring, they still owe an average of $188,000 in mortgage payments. This generation is in reasonably good financial shape because of their high credit scores and because they have lower rates of late payments than any other generation.

The Silent Generation is over 70 years, and most of them are long past their retirement age, and they live on their pensions and savings. Surprisingly, the homeowners in this generation still owe over $150,000 in mortgage payments, on average.

If you look at the personal debt situation across different countries, you will realize that the story is pretty much the same. People have easy access to credit, and they are able to make significant purchases when they are quite young, so they end up dealing with debt for the rest of their lives. Credit card companies and lenders across the world no longer care whether you are capable of paying back the credit limit they offer you because, for them, the incentive has changed—in many countries, lenders can auction off non-performing loans to debt collectors and then write off their losses, so they really have nothing to lose. Government regulators are often conflicted because they have to choose between helping their citizens gain access to credit and reigning in rogue creditors. Some governments are also heavily influenced by financial sector lobbyists, so they are unable to act effectively to stop things like subprime lending.

The bottom line is that from the moment you are able to take up some debt legally, there will be entities that will be more than willing to give you more credit than you actually need. You will find it very easy to start spending cash that you don't have on things that you don't need—and unless you are careful, you will quickly rack up a lot of debt.

In our modern society, lots of forces are working together to cultivate a consumerist outlook in you. From a very young age, you will be exposed to lots of media content that is tailor-made to turn you into a mindless consumer. You will see the glamorous lifestyles of celebrities—as well as the expensive clothes, cars, and houses in music videos—and you will decide that when you grow up, you want to be *that* rich. This idea will be reinforced in you throughout your life so that by the time you are old enough to get your first job, money will be your biggest motivation. When your first paycheck comes in, you won't be thinking about keeping any of that money for future use—you will be thinking of the nicest thing that you can buy for yourself with that cash.

When you grow up in a society such as this, your whole life experience trains you to want to be rich—but nobody ever tells you that you could choose to be wealthy instead. If you have the wealth mindset, you will understand that you don't become wealthy by spending all your money the moment you get some. Alternatively, you would know that keeping your money, investing it, and only spending it on essential things is what will make you exponentially wealthy, in the long run.

Minimalism can help you create the wealth mindset. When you are a minimalist, you learn to live on as little as possible and to avoid wasting your money on things that you don't need, which means that you learn to keep the money that you make and to pay off your debts. Minimalism changes the way that you understand personal success, and it redefines the metrics by which you measure your personal wealth. As a result, minimalism makes wealth more attainable.

You, too, can learn how to attain real wealth by applying the principles of minimalism as you create your spending plan and by developing the self-discipline that you need to be able to stick to your budget.

chapter 1: minimalism

what is minimalism?

Minimalism is a fairly complex concept because it covers many facets of one's life, but there is a simple one-sentence definition that probably applies to all minimalist practices—in a nutshell, minimalism is "making a conscious effort to live only with the things that one really needs." That means getting rid of the excesses in life and only keeping the basic things that you can't do without. That is a very simple characterization of a very complex concept. Minimalism isn't something that you do one time—it's a lifestyle choice. Thus, to practice it correctly, you have to incorporate it into the decisions that you make on a day-to-day basis.

The first thing to understand about minimalism is that you need to be intentional about it. It is not something that comes naturally to most people, and you have to make a conscious effort to override some of your ingrained habits as a consumer or as a hoarder. In essence, when you practice minimalism, what you are doing is that you are forcing yourself to let go of the baggage in your life in order to have the freedom to live an improved and a more fulfilled life.

The classic example of a minimalist act is decluttering your space, cleaning it out, and donating the things that you don't need to the people who really need them. For instance, most people in first world countries have way more clothes than they need, and their closets are filled with items that they haven't worn or used for months or even years. When a person takes up minimalism, one thing they would have to do would be to remove all those clothes from their closets and decide which ones to keep and which ones to donate, sell, or throw out. Most people who are new to minimalism are often shocked to find out just how much stuff they have that they don't really need.

Minimalism is about regaining one's freedom and breaking loose from the consumerism mindset. The truth is that our modern world has turned us into consumers of unnecessary things, and we are often influenced through advertising and through social pressure to buy things we don't need in order to appear and feel successful. Minimalism is about breaking from the idea that material possessions can bring us happiness and social acceptance. Minimalism is a conscious choice against unnecessary consumption, and it's a choice that one has to make every day.

Minimalists often reduce their consumerist tendencies by trimming their wallets and getting rid of credit cards that they don't really need. When you are new to minimalism, you will have to take out your credit cards and all the loyalty cards that you have and start reviewing just how essential each one is. If you have cards that you need but don't use frequently, you would have to take them out and keep them somewhere safe. If you have loyalty cards for stores and businesses where you buy a lot of unnecessary things (like coffee loyalty cards), you would have to get rid of those. If you have too many credit cards and if all they have done is make you spend more than you need to, get rid of those as well. Usually, new minimalists are encouraged to get a pair of scissors, cut their cards, and throw them out.

Minimalism is also about breaking free from the mania of the modern world. In ordinary life, we are always in a hurry, always stressed out, always running around at a feverish pace, and always working endless hours—just so that we can make enough money to afford things that we don't really need. It's a constant rat race—and in the end, when we get the cash, we always spend it almost immediately and then get back.to looking for more. Minimalism seeks to break that cycle. It helps people to slow down a bit, to take stock of their lives, to rediscover their passions, and to learn to enjoy simple things.

For example, some minimalists go as far as getting rid of their smartphones, and instead, they opt to use simple phones that don't have lots of apps to distract them and to occupy too much of their time. By getting rid of smartphones, minimalists are able to have more quality time with the people in their lives, they are able to notice their surroundings a lot more, and they are able to focus on their work and other activities that they are genuinely passionate about, and this, in turn, increases their productivity.

In many ways, minimalism is a countercultural movement. Most people live their lives while striving to measure up to standards that are portrayed in the media and in pop culture. In our culture, we idolize celebrities, and the vast majority of people aspire to have lives like theirs. We try to dress the way celebrities do, act and talk like them, and buy the fancy things that they have. Minimalism is countercultural because it rejects all that, and it tries to redefine what we think of as an "ideal" life. Minimalism teaches people that instead of chasing fame, wealth and glamour, they should seek to live quiet and humble lives. It recognizes the fact that happiness cannot be found through the pursuit of material things, but it comes from learning to enjoy the simple things in life.

For example, minimalists are encouraged to consume less social media and entertainment content. Some minimalists reduce the amount of time they spend on social media, watching online videos, and watching entertainment news. They reduce the number of people (especially celebrities) that they follow online, and some go as far as quitting social media altogether.

Minimalism is an internal journey and not an external one. Although minimalists spend a lot of time downsizing and getting rid of things they don't need, the fact is that they do this, no to show people how immaterial they are, but to find inner peace and satisfaction within themselves. Organization experts and psychologists have long understood that when we get rid of external clutter, we develop clear minds, and this makes us less anxious and more fulfilled.

why is minimalism important?

It creates room for important things.

When you become a minimalist, you get rid of the things you don't need, and you create space in your life for what is most important. The issue with having a lot of possessions is that those possessions demand a lot of our attention and energy. They take our focus away from the areas in our life that should be a priority. If you have a lot of books cluttering your shelves, you might never get the time to read the books that are really important to you. Consider donating or selling the books you have already read or no longer have an interest in reading, to free up some space and streamline your reading plan.

It gives you a lot of freedom.

If you have ever seen the movie Fight Club, you might remember that line about how the things we own end up owning us. When you own a lot of things, or when you want to spend money buying certain things, those things deny you freedom in many ways. You are not free to enjoy life because you have the crippling worry of whether you will be able to afford the fancy things in life that you want. Think of something as simple as buying a car. If you are not a minimalist, you will want something elegant, luxurious and expensive so that everyone around you can see how classy and successful you are. If you are a minimalist, all you have to consider will be whether the car can actually do the job you are buying it for (that is to take you from point A to point B), whether it has a small footprint in terms of carbon emissions, and a high level of fuel efficiency. In this case, minimalism will give you freedom from high car payments, insurance payments, and maintenance that will otherwise tie up most of your disposable income.

It can improve your mental health.

Minimalism has several psychological benefits, and it can improve your overall mental health. Ordinarily, we spend a lot of time worrying about being able to keep up with everyone else, and this often leads to anxiety and depression. We get anxious about how people will perceive us if we don't have fancy things. We often tie our self-esteem to our material possessions, and we think that the more we own, the happier we will be. When you take up minimalism, your whole outlook on life changes so that instead of worrying about the things you don't own, you start concerning yourself with appreciating the little that you do own. Minimalism improves our mental health by taking a lot of stressors out of the equation.

Stress comes about when we feel overwhelmed by our responsibilities, and when our minds are perturbed by the people and the things that surround us. Clutter causes stress, and stress affects your mental health. Studies have shown that the stress hormone cortisol, significantly spikes when we are trying to sort through the clutter to find something we misplaced. When you become a minimalist, and you clear your space and abandon your materialistic ambitions, you will effectively reduce your stress levels significantly.

It allows you to focus on developing healthy habits and constructive hobbies.

When we are materialistic, our hobbies revolve around trying to acquire more possessions and to make ourselves look richer than we really are. That usually means that we spend a lot of time at the hardware store doing one home improvement project after the other. We are always re-tiling our bathrooms, replacing our wooden countertops with marble, repainting our picket fences, etc. When we become minimalists, we shift our mindsets, and we start developing healthier hobbies. Instead of spending a fortune remodeling a kitchen that is already perfect, you will be more inclined to start a small herb garden at the back of the kitchen or to take up yoga, or start a fitness regimen.

It gives you a clear mind.

When we have clear minds, we tend to think a lot better, make smarter decisions, and feel more peaceful and relaxed. Psychologists have discovered an interesting concept called "decision fatigue," which relates clarity of mind and our ability to make smarter decisions. This concept postulates that when we have a lot of decisions to make, we tend to get mentally exhausted, our minds become clouded, and we end up making poor judgments, whether at work, in school, or even in our personal lives. Many psychologists believe that if we want to avoid mental exhaustion, we have to reduce the number of unimportant decisions that we make daily and focus all our mental energy on making decisions that are crucial and consequential.

If you are a minimalist, you will have clarity of mind, because you won't have to deal with all of the trivial decisions that use up your mental energy. Imagine for a second that you are a highly materialistic person. When you get up in the morning, you have to decide which toothpaste to use, which body-wash products to use, what shampoo or conditioner to use, which towel or shower robe to use, which make-up to put on, which clothes to wear, which accessories to add, and which car to take to work that day. By the time you get to the office, where mental exertion is required, you have already made dozens of decisions, and your decision quota for that day may already be on the verge of getting depleted.

However, if you are a minimalist, you won't have to make most of those decisions, and even for those that you do have to make, you won't spend a lot of time and mental energy on them because they would be straightforward. You will have one type of toothpaste, one type of showering soap (preferably something that's multipurpose), a single towel or bathrobe, a few makeup items, a handful of clothing options, and one single car. Instead of spending a lot of time sifting through the closet to find the perfect outfit, you will only have a few to pick from, to begin with. By the time you get to the office, you wouldn't have made that many decisions, and you have the mental clarity to make better decisions where your work responsibilities are concerned.

If this theory sounds farfetched to you, then perhaps you should know that a lot of productive people have actually been applying it in their lives for years. When Barack Obama was president, he made sure his wardrobe was stocked with suits that looked almost similar so that he wouldn't have to waste time in the morning deciding which one to wear. Renowned tech leaders such as Mark Zuckerberg and Steve Jobs also have/had similar rules (Steve Jobs only wore black turtle necks, while Mark Zuckerberg only wears dark t-shirts and hoodies). The idea is that they won't have to waste time or mental energy deciding what to wear, so their minds remain clear throughout the day, and they only make decisions on things that really matter.

It makes you less afraid of failure.

The fear of failure is one thing that we all experience at some point in our lives. We are often afraid to carry on with some major decisions in our lives because we are worried that in case those decisions do not pan out, we could end up without money or material possessions. But, what if we take the fear of lacking money and material possessions out of the equation? In that case, it's more likely that we will have the courage to do more things and to realize our true potential.

It makes you more confident.

Minimalism makes us more confident. Confidence stems from our ability to be comfortable with who we are as people and to be proud of our own accomplishments, however small they may seem. When we are materialistic, we are often ashamed of the fact that we don't have as many material possessions as other people, and this has an adverse effect on our self-confidence. A materialistic person would be afraid to show up to social functions with a small budget-friendly car or to invite people over to his tiny apartment. A minimalist would confidently pull up in a tiny car at social functions, and wouldn't worry about having people over, no matter how small their apartment may be.

When you lack confidence, it affects you in many areas of your life. It can negatively impact your career because of your inability to comfortably network with people above you in the career ladder. It can impact your personal life in a way that you'll keep wanting to wait until you have more money before you start forming meaningful bonds with other people. Minimalism teaches you that it's okay not to have material things so you won't have to attach your self-worth to your net worth.

Minimalism can aid you in saving more money.

The ironic thing about having money and wealth is that the more you want to show people how much money you have, the less likely you will be to save enough money to be actually wealthy. When you are materialistic, your money will be spent almost as soon as your paycheck comes in (sometimes, your entire paycheck could even go into paying credit card bills). However, when you are a minimalist, many of your expenses will disappear. You won't have to deal with high car and mortgage payments so you will be able to save most of your money. A few years down the line, you will actually be worth more than your counterparts who are obsessed with physical symbols of wealth.

who can benefit from being a minimalist?

Minimalism can be beneficial to the following groups of people in the following ways:

Children

Children can benefit from minimalism in many ways. First, minimalism can be the key to stopping children from growing up into materialist adults who manage their cash poorly. Children need to learn from a young age that having a lot of material possession isn't going to make them happy and fulfilled. Minimalism also teaches kids how to live comfortably with fewer possessions, and this can help them learn to live within their means as adults. It also teaches kids to think a lot more carefully about the things that they buy, and to know what their priorities are. Minimalism can teach kids to be creative. For example, instead of buying expensive toys for kids, they could learn certain crafts, and they might even learn how to make their own toys. Minimalism also teaches kids to be organized and clutter free from a very young age, and this is an important habit that could be beneficial to them for the rest of their lives.

Teenagers

The teenage years are very crucial in a person's development because this is the first time that most people encounter peer pressure, and the need to fit in and to be accepted by others. Most people start developing consumerist tendencies at that age. That is when most of us start obsessing over having nicer clothes, cars, and other possessions. As a parent, you may be able to teach your teenagers to become minimalists by making them pay for the more expensive items they want, so they learn a realistic and deeper understanding of the correlation between work, consumerism, and money. If you buy your teenage child an expensive first car, he or she will get used to high-end cars, and it will register in his or her mind that possessions are important. If you make your teenage child work for the cash to buy their car (even if you offer to pay a certain percentage) they will realize that it's truly hard to make money, and they may even settle for a reliable used car. He or she will understand those expensive items aren't that important after all.

Young Adults

Most young adults are usually living on their own for the first time, so they'll be fully in charge of their own budgets, their own welfare, and their own lifestyle choices. At the same time, young adults are usually at the start of their careers, or just finishing college so their income will be somewhat limited. Young adults, particularly millennials, are increasingly adopting the minimalist lifestyle, mostly for economic reasons. Millennials, especially those living in major cities and towns, are finding that renting large houses is quite expensive, so many of them are sharing costs with close friends, while others have begun renting 'micro-apartments.'

Minimalism can be extremely beneficial to young adults because it can help them navigate an economically challenging stage in their lives, and it can enable them to live with whatever little they have and to develop healthy financial habits such as budgeting and saving.

The Elderly

Minimalism can also be beneficial for the elderly in lots of different ways. Most elderly people have worked their whole lives, and some of them may have already paid off their houses, and they may be living on a fixed income, or on their savings. Their children may already be adults with families of their own, so they don't need the extra space in their houses. Elderly people have a lot of reasons to downsize and to declutter. They can sell their homes and move into smaller houses in warmer areas. They can sell their possessions to have a little bit more cash for their retirement. They can even downsize so that they have some extra cash to go on a cruise or to travel to exotic destinations. Minimalism is also a great thing for elderly people who are beginning to lose their memory, because the fewer things they have, the easier it is to organize their spaces and to locate their important belongings.

Entrepreneurs

Minimalism can be a great philosophy for entrepreneurs for several reasons. When you are an entrepreneur, you will need no distractions so that you can focus on your business, and minimalism can help you with that because it simplifies your life. Minimalism can also help you come up with a lot of creative ways of reducing your business startup or running costs. For example, if you are a minimalist, you learn to make do with affordable office equipment and furniture instead of spending a big chunk of your starting capital on fancy state-of-the-art office equipment. Minimalist entrepreneurs may also opt to use cloud storage for their files instead of wasting paper printing every document just to end up with lots of clutter on their desk. Minimalists use the simple approach to most things so they may be better at managing their time and reducing stress, which are qualities that make one a better entrepreneur.

Career People

People who are in various careers can also benefit from minimalism. If you apply minimalism in the projects that you do at the office, you may be in a better position to manage costs and to reduce wastage of other resources. If you practice minimalism in your personal life, the qualities that you acquire could easily spill over to your work life, and this can help you advance in your career a lot faster than some of your colleagues.

It's important to note that minimalism teaches people to focus their efforts towards jobs that they are passionate about and to give more priority to personal fulfillment than just making money. Meaning, minimalism can help to set you on the right career path so that you don't have to waste years of your life on a job that doesn't fulfill you in any way.

Men

Minimalism can make you a better man. It can make you a better husband, boyfriend, father or friend. If you are a man, minimalism enables you to prioritize spending time with your loved ones over the pursuit of material wealth so it can help you have a better relationship with your significant other, and it can stop you from missing all of the important milestones in your children's lives. Minimalism will also help you manage your finances a lot better so that instead of wasting money on unnecessary things, you will be directing it towards the things that your family really needs (like retirement savings or college money for the kids).

Men find it difficult to take up minimalism because they love their toys (mostly fast cars or big trucks), and they are under a lot of social pressure to appear to be successful. Many men are obsessed with symbols of masculinity, and for most of them, adopting a minimalist lifestyle would require a significant shift in their thinking.

Women

Although it's in decline, there was this popular misconception that minimalism was just for single guys who liked to backpack around the world without being attached to anything or anyone, but we now know that some of the most renowned minimalists are women. A lot of women have embraced minimalism to help them organize their spaces and to get rid of the things they no longer need.

Women have a difficult time embracing minimalism, especially when it comes to decluttering because most of them aren't too comfortable with giving up some of their perfectly nice clothes and shoes. Research shows that on average, women are more likely to save their items for future use than men. However, women are also more organized than men, and they are also more receptive of new self-improvement ideas.

How Do You Become a Minimalist?

Now that you understand what minimalism is and how you can benefit from embracing it, let's look at the essential steps that are involved when you decide to become a minimalist. As you go through these steps, remember that the aim is to declutter all areas of your life and that it's a complex process that will take quite a bit of time if you decide to implement it, but it's going to be worth it.

Evaluate your life and decide what your priorities are going to be.

Embracing minimalism means adopting a whole new lifestyle, so your first step would be to evaluate your life as it is and try to figure out what your real priorities are. You have to simplify your life, so you have to figure out what's really essential in every area of your life so that you know what things to retain and what things to get rid of. You have to list down all the things that make up most of your life and try to rearrange them in their order of priority. If you don't get your priorities straight, you may find yourself getting rid of something important and in its place, keeping something that you actually don't need.

Take a look at all your possessions and decide which ones you truly need.

The second thing you need to do is to take a look at all of your possessions and decide whether to keep them. Take your list of priorities and compare them with your possessions. If you have possessions that don't help you achieve any of your priorities, those possessions need to go. You also have to decide whether each possession actually adds value to your life, or if it just occupies space and distracts you from important things. Don't keep certain items just because they are nice to have. Make sure that you only keep the things that have practical and regular uses.

Assess how you spend your time.

Minimalism isn't just about getting rid of physical things. It's also about getting rid of activities that waste your time. You have to evaluate all the activities that you engage in, and then figure out if they are truly worth your time. If you don't evaluate your time, you may end up spending a lot of hours doing things that are fun at the moment, but they don't truly add any value to your life, or they may even be harmful in the long run. To evaluate how you spend your time, you can keep a log of all your activities for a while then use that data to analyze your time expenditure. When getting rid of time-wasting activities, it's advisable to start small and eliminate one activity at a time. Try replacing a night spent binge-watching your favorite series on Netflix with a family game night, or a date night with your spouse.

Evaluate the people with whom you spend your time.

You also have to look at who you spend time with and evaluate whether those people are really worth your time. Minimalism is also about getting rid of the toxic people in your life and giving priority to your most important relationships. You need to reallocate the time you spend with negative people, and you need to nurture your relationships with the people who build you up and add value to your life. If you spend too much time with negative people, you may start picking up their bad habits, so you need to make this change as fast as you can.

Set some boundaries and limits for yourself.

As you start out your journey as a minimalist, you have to understand that there are things that you won't be able to get rid of because they are ingrained in your personality, or they are essential to your work and your relationships. For example, as a minimalist, you may consider getting rid of your smartphone, but the fact is that you need it so that you can read your messages and work emails and respond to them promptly. You may want to cut out social media, but you may need it for marketing or for other work-related purposes. In such cases, you need to set boundaries for yourself such as limiting your time on social media to one hour a day, unless required for work.

Learn to do one thing at a time.

Part of minimalism is developing the ability to focus on important things and to get rid of things that aren't important. Towards that end, as you transition into a minimalist, and as you go on with your daily routines, you need to remember to focus on a single task at a time and to avoid multitasking. Multitasking is detrimental to productivity because it forces you to shift from one activity to the other without giving any of the activities your full attention. You are more effective as a minimalist if you do one thing at a time.

Revisit all your ambitions and goals.

You also need to revisit your goals and ambitions and reevaluate them to see if they are in line with your values as a minimalist. Some personal goals and ambitions may negate your efforts towards minimalism so it may be in your best interest to review them and to alter them so that you don't have any disharmony in your life. For example, if you have been saving up to buy a Porsche, and you have decided to embrace minimalism, you may have to change that dream into something that is in line with the principles of minimalism, for instance, you could turn those savings into a down payment for a beautiful little house.

Start with something small.

You have to remember that you don't just wake up one day and become a full-fledged minimalist. It's a lifestyle choice for which you have to work one day at a time until you become good at it and it becomes a habit. If you expect to turn into a minimalist overnight, you will be hugely disappointed. Instead, you should ease into it and try to make gradual but steady improvements.

Be more deliberate about how you live your life.

One significant component of minimalism is the ability to live in the moment and to avoid going through life on autopilot. You need to stop dwelling on the past and worrying too much about the future, and instead, focus all your attention into the things that you are doing at that very moment. The fact is that you won't be able to change the things that have already happened, and you can't control things that are yet to happen, so your best chance of making your life better is by giving the present moment all of your attention, and working hard to ensure that your future will be a little bit more comfortable.

Reduce your media and online content consumption.

We have already talked about setting limits for yourself, but it's worth mentioning on a separate point that a big part of minimalism is reducing the interference that tech gadgets have on our lives. When we consume a lot of media through all our smart devices, we waste a lot of time. More than that, media tends to implant a lot of consumerist ideas into our heads, and we are always tempted by adverts, celebrity lifestyles, and product placements. Whether its television, movies, online videos, social media photos, or even blogs, you need to reduce the amount of media you consume, and you need to spend more of your time reading books.

Factor minimalism into all of your future decisions.

As a minimalist, you need to factor minimalism into all the decisions that you make from this point onwards. Before you purchase something new, you have to examine your motivations for making that purchase, and you have to assess whether you truly need that item or whether your consumerist tendencies are creeping back into your mind. Keep working at minimalism every day, and don't bow to pressure from your friends to abandon your new lifestyle.

chapter 2: budgeting

what is a budget?

In the conventional sense of the word, we understand the term budgeting to mean how individuals or entities can estimate their expenses and try to match those expenses with the revenue that they have. However, for the purposes of this book, we will take a more holistic view of that term. When we talk about a budget, we don't just mean a plan on how to spend your money. The fact is that besides finance, there are other resources that one can budget for. Aside from financial budgeting, we will also look into how a person can budget his or her time or how he or she can create a budget that is based on his or her own personal values.

Personal Finance Budgeting

Individuals, couples, and families need personal finance budgets to be able to have a stronger grip on their expenses. It is easy to assume that only people with low income should have budgets, but that is a misconception that we need to dispel. Even if you have a large paycheck coming in every week and even if you have enough savings in your accounts to last you a lifetime, you still need to budget to manage that money effectively. Don't assume that just because you are well off, you cannot benefit from a personal finance budget. A lot of people assume that budgeting is not for them and that they can flourish without one—so let's unpack some of the assumptions that people make so that you can understand why you might need a personal finance budget of your own.

When you make enough money to cover all of your essential expenses, including all your bills and groceries, you can easily assume that a budget is not for you—but that isn't the truth. You, too, need a budget because when spending becomes an open-ended thing, expenses are going to creep in from nowhere. Let's say that you have $500 in disposable income after paying all the bills and that you haven't allocated that money any specific function. What you have is "idle money," and it's going to be an itch at the back of your mind—so anytime you turn on the TV and see an infomercial, you are going to be thinking, "Why don't I just buy that? I certainly can afford it!" You will go online and scroll through e-commerce sites, and every item on those sites will be a temptation. When you have a budget, you will be able to assign a specific duty to each and every dollar in your bank account—and whenever you are tempted to spend cash on anything nonessential, you will be more inclined to reconsider your options because it would mean that you are taking cash away from something else.

Lots of people also fail to budget for their cash because they assume that budgeting requires a lot of math skills. You may have come across a person who says that he or she can't budget because "I'm just not a numbers guy." Many people shy away from budgeting because they are unwilling to sit down and start punching numbers into a calculator. If you are one of those people, the good news for you is that now, we have lots of free and affordable accounting software and apps that are optimized for personal financial management and for budgeting. You can easily install one of those apps on your computer and use simple templates to input your expense and income values so that you can easily build your budget from there.

Another misconception that people have that stops them from creating a personal finance budget is the assumption that they enjoy great job security and that they, therefore, never have to worry about having a constant flow of income. That assumption is often misguided because even if you are the best worker in your department, the fact is that no corporation stays stable forever, and there is always a chance that you could be laid off because of downsizing, or because of a merger that makes your job redundant. Small successful companies could get mismanaged, or they could even die off if the original owner retires or passes on. Budgeting and proper financial management can help you better deal with unforeseen circumstances that could cause you to lose your income.

People also assume that budgets will deprive them of the finer things in life, so they avoid budgeting all together so that they don't feel guilty when they make expensive purchases. The fact is that a budget isn't meant to guilt you into not buying nice things. It's just intended to help your account for your money a lot better. It enables you to deal with your priorities first so that secondary expenses can come in later. When you are making a budget of your own, you are at liberty to allocate a portion of your income to 'entertainment' or 'fun activities.' The most important thing is that you understand exactly how much you spend on those fun activities because if you don't take stock, you can quickly acquire run-away expenses that can hijack your finances.

The Process of Budgeting Your Time

As we said, budgeting is more than just about the finances. We could argue that budgeting for your time is more important than even budgeting for your money because while you can always make more money, you can never recover lost time. Budgeting for your time is about developing better time management skills. We will take a brief look at how you can create a time budget.

To create a time budget, you have to track the amount of time that you spend on certain activities. By tracking your time, you will be able to identify an area where you tend to waste it, and this can empower you to make real changes in your life. You might find that you spend a little too much time watching television, but not enough time reading.

Once you have identified areas where you waste time, you will have to identify the important things that you need to spend more time doing so that you can reallocate your time to those things. If you have activities that require a lot of brain power and concentration, it would be better for you if you scheduled them earlier in the day when you are generally more productive. Your time budget won't be similar to anyone else's because your priorities are unique to you. However, as a rule of thumb, you have to remember to allocate more time to things like work activities, spending time with your family, and academic studies. Leisure activities are encouraged because they help you unwind, but under no circumstances should they be a bigger priority than core activities that help improve your life.

When you implement your time budget, you need to train yourself to watch the clock very closely. You always need to be aware of what time it is, possibly to the nearest 5 minutes. The best way to manage your time is to review how you spend small chunks of it. For example, you may have allocated 2 hours for studying in the evening, but within those 2 hours, you need to monitor your work progress in smaller chunks. You have to ask yourself, "Have I been doing something productive in the last couple of minutes, or have I just been distracted?" Even if you have a well-appointed time budget, you can easily find yourself at the end of a scheduled session when you haven't completed the activity that you wanted to do. That is why you need to make smaller time budgets within your larger time budget. For example, if you have allocated 2 hours for studying a chapter of your textbook, you can break that down further and say for instance that you will be studying one page every 5 minutes.

Value-based budgeting can help ensure that the things on which you spend your time and money are in line with the values that you hold dear. When creating a value-based budget, you have to start as usual by tracking how you spend your time and money—then, you have to hold those things up to the values that you espouse and see if they actually measure up. You have to ask yourself, "Does this expense reflect my values?" or "Will spending this much time doing this particular activity help me reach my goals and foster my values?" If you find that an activity or an expenditure goes against values that are important to you, cut it out altogether, or find a substitute activity or expenditure that won't violate your values. For example, if you value minimalism, and you are considering spending cash or time on something that goes against the values that underlie minimalism, you may want to rethink your whole plan and find a way to substitute that activity or expenditure with something that will ultimately provide you the greatest value in the long run.

what are the benefits of having a budget?

Holistic budgeting can have numerous benefits for individuals, couples, and families. Unfortunately, most of us tend to avoid taking the time to do any of it because it feels like a chore. In this chapter, we will discuss why it's advantageous for you to go through the hassle of sitting down and coming up with a value based budget for your time as well as your money.

It gives you absolute control over your time and money.

One thing that you have to understand is that if you aren't controlling your finances, then they are controlling you. The same thing applies to time — if you aren't managing your time, then external forces will have control over your time. Having control over your life is essential because it enables you to be happier and to make decisions that are in your own best interest so that you don't feel as though you are a slave to external circumstances. When you have 100% control over your time and your money, you can spend both resources in a way that maximizes your happiness and your fulfillment. When you have control, you have the power to iron out all the weaknesses in your spending and your time management habits, and this makes you more productive and more successful.

It allows you to track your time-bound goals, including your financial goals.

Unless you have a budget, you won't be able to track some of your financial goals and other personal goals that are time-bound so you won't be able to monitor your progress. If you can't monitor your progress with certain goals, your chances of actually achieving your goal will be significantly diminished. Supposing you are trying to read a book, but you haven't created a time budget, and you haven't allocated specific chunks of time towards that effort. How will you know that you are taking too long? When it comes to your finances, suppose you are saving up for a down payment for a house, but you don't have a budget that allocates a certain amount of income towards that goal. How will you know that you are on track to meeting your goal? As part of your budget, you will write down all your goals, and this will enable you to allocate each goal enough time and money to make sure that it is realized.

It brings your attention to mistakes about which you may be unaware.

When you have a proper holistic budget, you will be completely aware of where your cash is coming from and where it's going. You will also be aware of how much time you have on your hands, and how you spend that time. This will help you understand what errors you are making in the way you spend your cash and your time, and you will, therefore, be able to make better judgments. If you know exactly how much disposable income you have after paying for all the essential items that you need for the month, you will know what you can afford and what you can't.

Understanding how much time you need to invest to accomplish certain goals can also help you understand whether or not you can afford to spend considerable amounts of time on trivial things.

It helps you to be more organized in how you spend your time and money.

Budgeting in a holistic way helps you to be more organized in your approach to all facets of your life. When you create a holistic budget, you will break down all your expenses and bills, including what you need to pay for insurance, your mortgage, car payments, internet access, etc. You may be able to print out a template for your personal finance budget, and it will help remind you to pay all your bills promptly. The same thing applies when you create a budget for your time. You will be more organized in the way that you perform your duties and fulfill your social obligations. A budget will also help you catch slight changes in your expenses that you might have missed if you didn't plan your payments. For example, your utility company might decide to raise its unit fee slightly, and this could result in a significant bump in your monthly bill. If you have a budget, you will notice that your bill exceeds your normal allocation, and you will be able to make adjustments. However, if you don't plan your budget, you may not notice that your expenses have gone up slightly, and this could be a major setback, especially if you fail to account for that slight change in your bill.

It can cushion you against unforeseen expenditure and events.

Proper budgeting includes setting aside funds for the purposes of emergencies. Life is unpredictable, and from time to time, unexpected expenses may come up. You have to prepare for such expenses by factoring them into your budget. Life can surprise you with things like a trip to the hospital, a plumbing issue at the house, or a mechanical problem with your car. When these things happen, you have to be prepared so that you don't have to take out a loan or use credit cards.

When budgeting your time, you also have to consider the occurrence of random events that could use up a lot of time. If you have major upcoming projects, it's wise to budget your time in such a way that you would be able to finish your project a little while before it's actual hard deadline. That way, if something unforeseeable happens, you would still be able to deliver on time. For example, if you are writing a book report for school, budget your time in such a way that you will be able to complete your book report a couple of days before its really due, so that in the event something interferes with your plans, you still have a day or two to make up for the lost time.

It can improve your personal relationships.

Our relationships are strained when we don't spend enough time with the people we love. The same relationships are also strained when we mismanage money, and financial problems become a source of tension. A holistic budget can help improve your relationships in several ways. First, it makes it possible for you to prioritize your time so that you can spend more quality time with the people you love. Second, it allows you to prioritize your spending so that all your money goes into relevant expenses, and this can significantly reduce the tension between you and your spouse or your family members.

Financial problems are one of the leading causes of divorce, and they can be truly damaging to all sorts of relationships. The problem with our society is that in some of our households, we think of financial discussions as taboo subjects. That is an unhealthy approach, so we need to be able to change our mindsets in order to reap the benefits of a well-planned budget.

It can help you create a safety net.

Budgeting can help you create a safety net of your own so that you have peace of mind and the ability to survive in case there are drastic shifts in your financial situation. The question you need to ask yourself is, "If I get fired today, how long will I be able to survive before I get my next job?" If you have a budget, then you have a full understanding of your income and expenses, and you have more money in your personal savings and in your emergency fund, so you will be able to hold yourself over when things get tough. Having a safety net can also help you transition into a more fulfilling career. For example, if you dislike your job, and you would like to start your own business, you will be more inclined to take the next step if you have enough money to cover your expenses for the next 6 months or more.

It can help you to pay off all your debts a lot faster.

Budgeting both your time and money can help you get your debt under control. Most adults have debts in areas such as car payments, student loans, mortgage payments, etc. Having a budget can help you to stay up to date with your payments, and it makes you less likely to default because you will be setting aside money from every paycheck to go into your debt payments. As you analyze your finances before creating a budget, you will have a better understanding of the terms of your loans, particularly your interest rates, and this can help you figure out how to regain control over those loans. For example, if you budget well and reduce your expenses in other areas, it could allow you to increase your monthly loan payments so that you are able to pay off the whole thing a lot faster and therefore pay less in interest in the long run.

If you budget your time well, you may be able to free up your time so that you can take extra shifts at work, get a second job, invest your money, or start a side business that can help you raise more money and pay off your debts a lot faster.

why is budgeting difficult?

The word 'budget' has a negative connotation in the minds of most people. We tend to think of budgeting as something negative. First of all, it requires us to apply mathematics, and the fact is that doing mathematical calculations isn't something that the average person enjoys. Even people who use math daily in their jobs have a negative view of budgeting because it just feels like more work to them. Some psychologists believe that the reason people dislike budgeting is similar to the reason why people dislike dieting. In the centers of the brain that control emotional responses, words like 'budget' and 'diet' are associated with things such as agony, suffering, depression, and the general feeling of being deprived of something. In other words, when words like 'diet' or 'budget' come up, our emotional brains immediately associate them with discomfort and hard times, and we immediately start thinking of those words as negative things.

Some psychologists believe that if you mention the word diet, to some people, it makes them feel as though there is a famine that is coming. While the body may be able to deal with a brief period of famine, it can't handle starvation in the long run, and that explains why most people end up dropping their diets after just a few days. When you are on a diet, even the foods that you ordinarily try to avoid, begin to look appealing and appetizing because the 'reward value' of food is significantly increased. That means that the longer you are on a diet, the harder it becomes to resist even the foods that you typically won't consider eating.

The same principle applies when you are dealing with a budget. When you start budgeting, you will be more tempted to make purchases than you are under ordinary circumstances. That's because you will feel as though making certain purchases is forbidden, so you will start obsessing over the things that you can't have. Once you get started on a budget, all the things that you are missing out on because of the budget will start popping into your head, and you will have a difficult time focusing on the benefits that you are expecting to gain from taking up that budget. When you make your own meals, you will start wishing you were out at a nice restaurant. When you drive your budget-friendly car, you will wish that you were in a large SUV. When you are on a budget, your emotional brain will tell you that you are dealing with scarcity, and you will feel the urge to spend some money so that you can put an end to that scarcity.

There are deep psychological reasons that make it difficult for us to stick to budgets, so when we are trying to start budgeting, we need to understand these psychological constraints so that we can make them work for us instead of letting them control us. The first psychological trick to use is changing the way we refer to budgets. Instead of making a budget, you need to create a 'spending plan.' The spending plan is similar to the budget in the sense that it's meant to accomplish the goal of making you more responsible for your finances. However, the difference is that although budgets focus on placing restraints on your spending, your spending plan will be focused on redirecting your resources towards helping you to achieve your most important goals.

When you want to start a spending plan of your own, you will sit down and create a list of the things that you value the most, as well as a list of the things you enjoy the most. You will make sure that you go into very specific details about those things, and that you understand everything that it would entail for you to achieve those things.

For example, if you would like to go on vacation to the Caribbean at the end of the year, you would make sure that you make that goal as vivid as possible. You would have to create visual images that could help you goal feel a lot more tangible. For example, you could get pictures from the place you want to visit and hang them in rooms where you spend most of your time. You could also use pictures of your destination as the background images on your phone, your computer, or your tablet. Once you've made your goal seem real and attainable, it's time to figure out how you intend to pay for it. You could start a plan to save enough money to achieve that goal. You could figure out what the goal is going to cost you, and find out how much money you would have to put aside each month to realize that goal within the predetermined time frame. You have to understand where the money will be coming from, what fraction of your income it is going to be, and how you are going to secure the money to avoid the temptation of spending it on other things. You also have to figure out what things you are going to forgo in order to have the money that you need to save. Budgets and spending plans are similar when it comes to implementation, and they only differ because of slight differences in their approaches.

Our ability to properly manage our money depends on our behavior, and slight changes in the way we approach personal finance management can have a massive impact on whether or not we would actually be able to control runaway spending in the long run. While budgets feel like painful constraints, spending plans make us feel as though we are in control of our own finances, and they even serve to motivate us to manage our money a lot better. When you use a spending plan in place of a budget, you will feel really excited about the fact that you will eventually get to spend cash on the things that you truly want, and you will feel a sense of satisfaction when you eliminate wasteful spending from your life.

Another psychological reason why we find it difficult to stick to budgets is that we are naturally more optimistic than realistic. That means that we often assume that we will spend money sensibly, and therefore we underestimate each line item in our budgets. Market researchers did a study where they asked people to guestimate their spending for the next month, and for the next year. What they found was that most people were bad at estimating their spending for the next month, but they were a bit better at guessing their spending over the whole year.

Those researchers stumbled upon something rather curious here. While you may assume that it's easier to estimate short term expenses than long-term expenses, the truth is that when we estimate short-term expenses, we tend to imagine that we would be more frugal. When we estimate long-term expenses, we understand the fact that because it's a long period of time, some unforeseen things will come up, so we tend to make higher estimates just in case. That is an important observation because it means that while we know that we have a tendency to overspend, we technically aren't conscious of it when it actually happens. In other words, most of us overspend unconsciously. It is that unconscious overspending that makes us break our budgets or spending plans.

Unconscious overspending occurs in different ways, and unless we make efforts to be more aware of them, we won't be able to stay within over spending plans. You may be pushing your cart down the supermarket aisle, picking up groceries, and then you spot a snack item that you really like. At that moment, you are going to think "a couple of dollars' worth of snacks certainly won't ruin my budget," and you toss that item into your cart. At that moment, it won't seem harmful, but the problem is that moments like that occur all of the time, and the cash tends to add up pretty fast.

Another way we overspend unconsciously is by going over budget on certain items by rounding off the figures mentally. Supposing you go to a shoe store with the intention of spending $300 on a pair of shoes. When you walk around, you see a perfectly nice pair at $280, but right next to it, there is a slightly nicer pair at $320. Which pair are you going to buy? You may tell yourself that either way, it is $20 give or take. More often than not, if you have the money, you may opt for the nicer pair. While that is fine, the problem is that you will make the same decision with every other item you buy that month, and in the end, you will realize that you are way over your budget.

When creating a spending plan, it's better to overestimate your spending so that you have some wiggle room, and you don't feel too constrained to the point that you are tempted to abandon the plan altogether. You should also keep track of your spending, and try to take note of the number of times within each month that you experience a spending dilemma similar to any of the ones that we have discussed above.

Another psychological reason why we tend to overspend is that we do a lot more of our transactions electronically, so it doesn't really register in our minds that we are losing cash. Psychologists have found that when we use credit cards, debit cards, and online payment platforms such as PayPal and Apple Pay, we tend to spend more than we would when we use cold hard cash. In a study done by researchers at MIT, it was discovered that people were willing to spend 2-thirds more on tickets to certain events if they paid electronically versus if they paid with cash. When you hand over cash to someone, that transaction feels a lot more tangible, and the sense that you are losing something of value registers in your mind. When you buy something electronically or even online, you don't actually give away anything physically, so there is no moment of hesitation where you stop to give the whole thing a second thought.

Stores and retail companies understand this concept. That is one of the reasons why so many of them are in the process of phasing out cash payments as an option. However, as long as you can, you should try to make cash payments whenever you make a purchase, even though it may feel like a bit of a hassle every time you have to go out to find an ATM machine.

Another reason why budgeting is so difficult is that psychologically, there is some disconnect between our present and our future selves. This applies to personal finance and budgeting as well as in many areas of our lives where we have to work hard for something. Budgeting requires you to spend less money presently so that you have the cash to spend in the future. However, we have a natural inclination to think of our future self as someone else who is a stranger to us. Saving for the future can sometimes feel as though we are keeping the money so that someone else can use it.

One final reason why we have a difficult time sticking to our budgets is that we set goals that seem big and distant, so it always feels as though we will have ample time to deal with our money problems much later. For example, let's say that you are in your late 20s, and you tell yourself that you want to save a million dollars for your retirement. At that age, you have at least 30 more years in the workforce, so you are likely more inclined to spend whatever you make now and instead start saving cash in a couple of years. The days will go by fast—and by the time you are in your late 30s, you will be underperforming, and your motivation will die off. However, if you break that savings goal down into smaller bits, you may find that it's more manageable. For instance, you could decide that you want to save $70,000 before you are 30, $200,000 before you are 35, and so on until you get to your goal. You could even break it down much further until you know exactly how much you need to save this month or even this week to reach your goal by the time you retire.

chapter 3: minimalist spending plan

what is minimalist spending really about?

As a minimalist, you have to spend money on things that provide value and real purpose to your life, as well as things that give you freedom. We've mentioned that when you spend too much on things that you don't need, you become a slave to consumerism. For minimalists, spending is about breaking the chains of consumerism and having the freedom to only pay for what helps us achieve goals that are aligned with our values.

Before you become a minimalist, you are primed to think of money as the most important thing in life. They tell you that money makes the world go round and that you should spend almost all of your waking hours looking for more of it. As a result of this mentality, you often end up prioritizing money over everything else in your life. You work long hours, and you forget to nurture your relationships with the people that are most important to you. You spend endless hours hunched over your desk, and you forget about your own health. All that's important is making money.

The problem, however, is that when that money finally comes in, the world tells you something different. Although the world wants you to work tirelessly to get money, it doesn't encourage you to keep it or to be more responsible with it. Instead, you are bombarded with messages about things that you should buy and lifestyles that you should aspire to have. As soon as you make a single dollar, there is a long line of wants in the back of your mind because companies have been working hard to make sure that your mind is wired that way. There is never a shortage of things to spend money on. Even things that you have that work perfectly well are soon phased out so that you have to buy newer and shinier versions of the same things. In the end, you are stuck in a vicious cycle of working hard to make money and then turning around to fork it over to companies and brands in exchange for things that you very well can do without.

Minimalist spending is really about breaking that cycle and freeing you once and for all. It's about overhauling your mindset so that, for the very first time, you can see the things that are really important to you and understand that possessions don't add value to your life. Even if you are good at the game of life as it is, you will never be truly happy until you break out of that cycle. Supposing that you are smart, you work hard and make a lot of money, so you can afford to pay for all the finer things in life. If you are a consumerist, you will never win because there is always another level of the same game ahead. If you can afford to buy a house, there is always the temptation to buy a second vacation home. If you can buy a high-end sports car, there is always the temptation of owning a yacht. In other words, no matter how good you are at it, consumerism has no end—and the only way to win is to stop playing.

There is a common misconception that minimalism encourages people (mostly young people) to be lazy, to avoid exerting themselves, and to stop participating in the economy.

Nothing could be further from the truth. All minimalism does is that it challenges you to rethink your priorities and to understand what's really important in life.

Minimalist spending is about using your income to buy your freedom instead of wasting it on consumerist trappings. It encourages you to think of money as something that you could use to free yourself. For example, let's say that someone handed you $500. How much freedom could you buy with that? For most people, if you had five hundred dollars, and if there was no risk of losing your job over it, you would probably take a couple of days off and do something fun. Now think of retirement. When you save money for retirement, you are essentially putting money away so that you could use it in the future to buy yourself some freedom. The easiest way to understand why money can be equated to freedom is by thinking of the lottery. What if you won $50 million in the lottery today? Would you still spend time doing a minimum wage job? You would probably quit that same day because money gives you the freedom to do what you really want. That is why when you spend money on things you don't need, you are essentially throwing away small chunks of your freedom.

Joshua Fields and Ryan Nicodemus are thought leaders when it comes to minimalist spending. They once suggested that when you want to make a certain purchase, you have to try to convert the cost of that item into 'freedom,' and then try to figure out if it's worth it. For example, if you walk into a clothing store and you are tempted to purchase an item that is worth $40, you have to ask yourself, "Is this piece of clothing worth $40 of my freedom?" When you look at it from that angle, you realize that the money is worth more than just its dollar value. It's also worth your time and your freedom.

Minimalist spending is about trying to keep yourself from getting shortchanged every time you spend money on fancy things that you can easily live without. For example, when you spend $30,000 on a car right now, you are not just losing a sizable chunk of your paycheck which will go into the car payments, you are probably also losing 2 whole years of freedom that you could have enjoyed when you retired.

Minimalist spending is about putting an end to the wastage of money. You could argue that all types of spending plans serve to reduce the wastage of money, but the fact is that minimalist spending goes a step further. It changes your understanding of what 'waste' really is, and it makes it possible for you to prioritize your freedom so that you aren't stuck in a lifelong trap of consumerism.

psychology of consumerism and purchasing

Consumerism is a complex issue, but the first thing that you need to understand is that without it, Western economies wouldn't be anywhere close to where they are today. From an academic standpoint the term consumerism refers to a theory which postulates that when we increase our consumption of goods, we boost the economy. However, the term consumerism is mostly used to refer to the human habit of spending money and other resources on things that aren't essential for human survival.

If you really think about it, consumerism is detrimental to an individual, so by definition, it should be considered to be a vice. However, our societies accept it, and they even extol it as a virtue. The government encourages consumerism because it facilitates economic growth. When you see the consumer index going down, macroeconomists start to worry, and the people in charge start crafting strategies to make people spend more. The point is that consumerism is one of the most psychologically confusing vices because while you have to go against social pressure when you take up vices such as smoking, society actually encourages you to consume more. As such, consumerism becomes a problem that most people don't even recognize as one.

One of the main psychological effects of consumerism is that it teaches people that "more is better." You always hear about offers such as "buy one get one free" and "get a free item on your 10th visit." When you come across such things, the idea that you should always be on the lookout for more material things becomes ingrained in you. Your motivation becomes to work hard, to earn money, to buy things, and to become happy as a result of having those things.

There are several problems that come about as a result of that mentality. The first one is that people are no longer intrinsically motivated to do anything. It used to be that people would travel across oceans, journey into jungles, go to foreign lands, study art, music and science, and they would do all these things because they were curious, and they had the spirit of adventure. Now, most people do the things they do because they just want to make enough money to afford the nice things in life. When we talk to our kids about their future prospects, we suggest career paths that we understand to be the most lucrative in terms of financial rewards, irrespective of what passions the child may have. Not many people want a job where they get to impact other people's lives. Everyone wants a job that pays the highest. Even when we have jobs in which we are well trained and perfectly competent, most of us would still jump at the opportunity to do something else if it paid just a little bit more.

Another problem with consumerism is that it's absolutely destroying the planet. Companies are always looking to churn out products so that they can sell more and make more money, and in most cases, they use up natural resources and release waste into the environment. Consumerism not only ruins our mental health, but it also threatens our very existence as a species.

Psychologically speaking, we shop to fulfill certain emotional needs. Consumerism is, therefore, a habit that we develop as a form of 'therapy' to help us deal with certain emotional shortcomings. For example, if you have an emotional need to be respected or to be admired by the people around you, you may go out and buy nice things so that you may be perceived as successful and affluent, and so that you may gain the respect that you want. In other words, we buy things to fit in.

The real tragedy of consumerism is that it actually works, albeit temporarily when it comes to fulfilling those emotional needs. As a result, it registers in our brains that we are doing the right things even though we are not. Let's say you walk into a store and you buy them a nice and expensive pair of shoes. You wear that pair of shoes to work or to a social gathering. You receive compliments from your friends and colleagues about those shoes, and everyone wants to know how expensive they are and where you bought them. At that moment, you are happy because your negative spending decision is receiving positive reinforcement from society.

When you wear reasonably priced shoes the next day, no one seems to pay attention to you, so the good action that you have taken isn't reinforced or encouraged in any way. When you need to buy a pair of shoes again in the future, you will know that you are better off financially if you get reasonably priced shoes, but you will also remember how great you felt when you bought the more fashionable pair, and you may, therefore, make the decision to pay more for a second shot at that temporary happy feeling. In a nutshell, that is how consumerism becomes ingrained in us like a habit.

Psychologically speaking, consumerism is essentially an addiction, and it can eat away at all your financial resources, destroy your hope, and negatively impact your wellbeing. Consumerism is like a drug that everyone encourages you to take. If you developed a meth habit, your friends and family members will hold an intervention for you and encourage you to seek help. If your consumerism gets out of hand, most people will encourage you to keep going on (either directly or indirectly), and the only way anyone would notice that it's a problem is if you are using their money. The only people who will ever tell you to stop overspending are; your spouse (if your habit is ruining their finances) and your parents (if you are still using their credit cards). Otherwise, nobody will ever bother to point out that your consumption habits are getting out of hand because they too don't want to be seen as people who are concerned about not being able to afford nice things.

You may have heard about shopaholics (or you may even be one yourself). These are people who are compulsive shoppers. They respond to stressful stimuli by shopping. When something happens to make them a bit stressed, anxious or depressed, they get their credit cards and go out shopping, or they log into e-commerce sites and start placing orders for things that they don't really need. Shopaholics are extreme versions of consumerists, but their habit is actually more dangerous because shopaholics actually lack impulse control. The term "oniomania" was coined as a name for the disorder that shopaholics have. While most consumerists may be able to reason their way out of making certain unwise purchases, shopaholics may not be able to do it because for them, it's a compulsive disorder, and it's very difficult for logic to win out over disorders that result from emotional reactions.

The consumerism problem is compounded by the fact that it is very easy for a person to spend money that they don't even have. Companies and businesses understand that we are more careful with money that we have worked hard to earn, so they have made it extremely easy to you to spend money that you are yet to earn, and then to pay for it later. As we have mentioned in this book, there is a disconnect between our present self and our future self, so it's easy for us to make mistakes at the present moment and then stick our future selves with the responsibility of fixing those mistakes.

When we use credit cards to buy things, or when we use loan money to pay for major purchases, it doesn't fully register in our minds that we are spending a lot more than we might be able to deal with, because there is a primal part of us that feels as though we a getting something for free. That's is why it's so easy for shopaholics to rack up thousands of dollars in credit card debt over a single weekend when they know pretty well that they would have to work for months or even years just to pay off those debts.

It's important to understand the psychology of consumerism so that you know what you are up against when you try to stop spending your hard earned money on the things that you don't need. You have spent your whole life getting the values of consumerism embedded in your brain, so you have to understand that it will be difficult to change your mindset in order to become a minimalist spender. You have to retrain your brain to understand that the upscale lifestyle that you are working so hard to pay for is not going to make you happy, and it's probably not going to be worth your while. It's going to be hard to understand that when you spend your time looking for and caring about physical possessions, you are wasting valuable time that you could be spending on creating stronger and more meaningful relationships with the people in your life. It's going to be challenging to accept the fact that with every unnecessary purchase you make, you are contributing to the demise of our planet.

However, the more you learn about minimalism and the more you practice it as you spend your money, the more you will notice that you are happier and under less pressure—and you will realize that the acquisition of material things isn't what life is about.

steps to creating a minimalist spending plan

Let's discuss in detail the steps that are involved in creating a minimalist spending plan.

Creating a Mindset That Prioritizes Financial Freedom as a Way of Decluttering

Applying minimalism to personal finance means decluttering your finances so that you have some financial freedom, and are not overly dependent on financial institutions and services such as bank loans and credit card services. In many households, a lot of stress and confusion arises from having too much financial clutter. Unlike ordinary clutter, financial clutter can prove to be quite stubborn when you want to get rid of it. When we talk about financial clutter, we are not referring to the paperwork that you have from your financial institution. Financial clutter has little to do with your banking documents, insurance forms, tax filling forms, credit card paperwork, and investment documents. Sure, those documents are important because you will need them as you try to unpack your financial clutter, but when we speak of financial clutter, we mean the financial mess that you might be in as a result of the choices that you have made regarding money.

If you want to be a financial minimalist, it helps if you think of things like loans, credit card accounts, bill payments, investments, savings, and personal expenses, as financial clutter. The way you handle clutter is the same, whether you are dealing with a messy closet or a messy financial situation. When you clean out your closet, you are trying to get rid of unnecessary things, remain with the bare essentials, and regain the freedom that you lose when you have too much stuff to worry about. With financial clutter, the end goal is almost the same. You need to get rid of unnecessary things that cause confusion like too many credit cards and too many small loans from different providers. You need to work towards simplifying things so that you only remain with the most essential financial obligations to worry about, and you need to regain the freedom that you lose when you owe money to a lot of people and when you work tirelessly to make money only to spend it on things you don't need.

The pursuit of freedom from material possessions is the foundation of minimalism. Your biggest priority as a financial minimalist will be to strive to be free from the kind of financial problems that you end up losing sleep over. The question then becomes, "How do you manage your finances in a clutter-free way?" Many steps are involved in that process, but your biggest priorities should be to reduce your debts, manage your income better, reduce your expenses, and increase your income and savings.

You need to ask yourself; "Which financial management methods make it easier for me to do all things in the easiest, fastest and simplest way?" It would be best if you considered going digital and making use of software or banking options that allow you to manage all your finances in one place so that you can automate most of your transactions.

You also need to create a practical and actionable spending plan, and you need to find ways to ensure that you will stick with that plan even when things get tough. Your plan should help you reduce your debts as well as your number of debtors so that you aren't confused at all times about which debtors to prioritize. You also need to come up with a plan for when you retire. That means that as you declutter your finances, you also save enough money, not spend it all as it comes in. You can only manage to do all these things if you are motivated and if you have the correct mindset towards achieving financial freedom.

You have to get into the mindset of consolidating things instead of letting them lie all over the place. In your personal finances, this means that you have to consolidate things like insurance policies, debts, savings accounts, and bill payments.

Financial minimalism also means that you deal with things promptly, and you don't waste time waiting for them to start accruing extra charges. That means that you may have to move things around so that you can make loan repayments and bill payments as soon as possible. If you are a renter, it also means paying your rent on time.

To prioritize your financial freedom, you have to understand the things that matter the most to you, and you need to have clear financial priorities. That means that you first have to understand your own personal values and to make sure that as you go about decluttering your finances, all of the decisions that you make should be in line with those values.

Goal Setting

When you set financial goals as a minimalist, you have to ensure that those goals are in line with the core principles of minimalism. When you are dealing with goals related to home ownership, your financial goal shouldn't be to buy the biggest most luxurious house you can find, but it should be to buy a decent enough house that is going to serve all the purposes that you need it to. As long as you remember not to negate the principles of minimalism in your goal setting process, you are at liberty to prioritize your own preferences.

The first thing in the goal-setting process is to figure out what is most important to you. You have to get some writing material and list down all the things that you know you want out of life at that point. It doesn't matter how serious or how ridiculous a wish is. As long as it's a wish that you have, it should make it to the preliminary list. The purpose of this exercise is to know all the goals and dreams that you have before you can begin to apply logic and principle to each one of them. It doesn't matter how soon you wish to achieve a goal, or how far into the future you expect to accomplish it. At this stage in the goal-setting process, everything is fair game.

The second thing you need to do is to put all your goals through the 'minimalism test.' That means that you have to weigh each goal that you have listed down and see if it negates the core principles of minimalism. If one of your goals is to own the newest model of your favorite smartphone which is to be launched in a couple of months, when you subject that goal to the minimalist test, you would have to ask questions like; Is this an item I need, or is it something that I just want? Does my desire to own this item stem from a consumerist mindset, or does this item serve a practical purpose in my life? Do I already have something else that does the exact thing that this item will be doing? The point of these questions is to help you understand whether the motivations for each one of your goals are based on practical consideration, or if they are based on a desire to keep up with the Joneses. Try to be as objective as possible, and strike out all the goals that aren't minimalistic in nature.

After that, you will have a shorter list of minimalistic goals, which you actually intend to achieve. At this stage, you will have to create a new draft of your list of goals, except that this time, you will sort your remaining goals depending on a rough time frame. You can either categorize them as long and short-term goals or break them down further depending on the range of time within which you expect to accomplish them (e.g., you can set goals to achieve within the month, within the year, within five hours, within 20 years, etc.).

The next thing you need to do is to apply the SMART strategy to your goals in order to gauge their viability. For your goals to be considered as SMART, they have to be Specific meaning they have to be clearly stated without any ambiguity as to what they mean. Measurable - there has to be an objective, empirical way in which you or someone else could assess whether or not you have actually achieved that goal. Achievable - the goals have to be realistic given the facts of your current situation, otherwise, you would be wasting your time on a pipe dream. Relevant - the goals have to fit within the grand picture of your life, and they shouldn't be standalone goals that aren't part of something bigger. Timely - your goals should be time-bound, meaning you have set a time frame for when you intend to achieve the goal or to reach certain phases while you are in the pursuit of your goal. If your goals fit these criteria, then it means that you are on the right path.

The next step in the goal-setting process is to figure out what you will need to achieve each one of your goals in terms of financial commitment, time commitment, and the commitment of other resources at your disposal. If your financial goal is to save money for a down payment on a home, you have to figure out how much money you need, and how much time you have, then work backwards to find out how much you need to save today, tomorrow and the day after that if you want to meet your goal.

After you have figured out the cost of achieving each one of your goals, you have to create a spending plan that will help you set aside the money you need to finance each one of your goals within the time-frame that you have set. Create a separate account aside from your normal transactional account, and use this account to set aside cash that is earmarked to bankroll all your goals, to make sure that you achieve each one of them.

Finally, you need to create a system that will help you monitor your progress and know how well you are performing in your pursuit of each one of your goals. When you are done with the goal-setting process, create a simple document that records all the details of your goals - update this frequently as you chip away at achieving the goal and always refer back to it to make sure that you stay the course and eventually accomplish each goal.

Identifying Your Spending Habits and Consumption Behavior

You need to take stock of all your spending and consumption habits and try to figure out which ones need the most work so that you can get rid of them and try to be more frugal. If you embrace minimalism, you will have an easier time figuring out which spending habits are need work, because you will start training yourself to identify the things in your life that you can do without.

To identify poor consumption habits, you can bring out all the receipts that you have collected over the past few months, lay them out and go through them one item at a time. As you read through your receipts, you have to ask yourself two simple questions. First, ask, "Could I have done without this item altogether?". Then, if you really did need the item, ask, "Could I have done just as well with a cheaper item?" If your answer is yes to one or both of those questions, then it means that you could have saved the whole amount or a fraction of the amount of money that you spent on that item. Take note of that item, as it is one brick on the wall of your poor spending and consumption habits.

One common poor spending habit that most of us have is the choice to buy branded products in places where generic products can easily suffice. Brand products are often more expensive than generic ones because companies have to pass the cost of branding and advertising on to the customer. There are certain areas where you lose something in terms of quality when you pick a generic item over a branded one, but in most areas, you will just be losing money paying for the brand premium.

Supposing for example, you go to the store to pick up a 5-pound bag of rice. You find that the generic bag costs $3 while your favorite brand costs $3.50. Which one are you going to pick? You may feel attached to your favorite brand, but you know for a fact that it's the same rice of the same grain type, produced through the same process, and meeting the same hygienic standards. The only difference is the packaging. The principles of minimalism dictate that you pick the more cost-effective option and you avoid unnecessary expenditure. It's estimated that you can save an average of 20 percent of the cost of all items if you opt for generic rather than branded items.

There are things that we are so accustomed to paying for to the point that sometimes, it doesn't register in our minds that they are actually unnecessary purchases. Let's take the example of bottled water. Some of us are so used to bottled water that we have forgotten that tap water is just as good in terms of physical, chemical, and biological qualities. Most cities and states have high water-quality standards that are strictly enforced, which means that tap water is clean enough to drink, so bottled water is an unnecessary expense. Did you know that if you drink the daily recommended 8 ounces of water every day, it could cost you an upward of $1000 a year if you prefer bottled water, and less than $1 over the same period if you prefer tapped water?

There are also numerous other ways we spend money unnecessarily without even noticing it. When we purchase items such as electronic appliances, it's okay to get a standard warranty, but extended warranties are generally a waste of money. When we are late on payments, and we have to pay late fees—that counts towards poor spending. When we pay to dry clean clothing items that are perfectly fine to wash, that is a luxury that we could do without.

The thing to remember about poor spending habits is that you lose a small and seemingly insignificant amount of money with every purchase, so it's easy to ignore those habits and assume that they are inconsequential. The problem is that those additional charges accumulate and we end up losing a lot of money in the process. You should always be looking for ways to iron out your poor consumption habits and to cultivate good ones in their place.

Simplifying Your Accounts and Consolidating Your Loans

Minimalism is about simplicity, so it is wise to simplify your accounts and your loans by consolidating them. You do need several accounts because you have to have separate checking, savings and maybe emergency accounts, but you should avoid having duplicate accounts serving the same purpose, such as two separate checking accounts. As a minimalist, it is important to consolidate most of your loans to avoid the hassle of dealing with multiple loan payments every month.

There are a lot of reasons to consolidate your accounts, especially when you are dealing with savings, retirement, and investment accounts. For starters, it is easier to manage one single account than it is to manage different accounts at different banks. You will have an easier time controlling your whole portfolio, and you won't waste too much time going from account to account when you need to keep track of your cash and your investments. When it's all in one place, it is easier to execute certain investment decisions without having to deal with bank transfers.

Secondly, you will pay less in terms of maintenance fees because fees are charged per account, and not according to your balance. When you have a lot of accounts, fees and commissions will add up fast, and they will eat into your savings. Many service providers offer breaks in fees and commissions when you reach certain thresholds, and that means that you are more likely to enjoy such benefits when you pool most of your cash into one account.

Consolidating your accounts also makes it easier for you to come up with a financial plan. When you plan for your retirement and major purchases, you get a better picture of your financial situation if you have your resources in one place, and you will be in a better position to come up with a more effective plan. If you try to make a plan while your money is spread over multiple providers, you fail to get a realistic view of your total resources and your cash flow situation, which can likely lead to miscalculations within your plan.

Consolidating your accounts is a good thing, but you have to be very careful and very wise when you do that. In some cases, it can mean that you have to liquidate the investments that you have made with some providers and that could have some tax implications (you might be required to pay Capital Gains Tax), so you have to make sure that it's actually in your best interest to consolidate each particular account. If you stand to lose a lot of money when you close certain accounts, it may be wise to keep those accounts open.

Consolidating your loans can help you to reduce your financial clutter and to create a more straightforward spending plan. One main advantage of consolidating your loans is that you only get to make one single monthly payment, so you don't have to waste time keeping track of multiple loans from different providers and sending out numerous payments each month Consolidation is especially good if you have lots of student loans. Some students graduate with more than ten different loans, and it can be confusing and overwhelming to try to service each one of those loans at the same time. When you consolidate these loans, they make up one-line items in your spending plan, so it becomes easier for you to figure out how to earmark cash to pay for it. Consolidation also reduces your chances of missing payments and ruining your credit in the process.

Loan consolidation opens up doors for alternative payment plans. If you consolidate your student loans in one place, you may be able to opt into payment plans such as the extended payment plan, the income contingent payment plan, or the graduated payment plan. Depending on your income, it may be advantageous for you to consider restructuring your loan and using a different repayment plan, but that only works properly when you have them all in one place. As a point of caution, you should be careful with some repayment plans because they may provide temporary relief end up causing you to pay a lot more in interest in the long-run.

Loan consolidation can also help you by making it possible for you to get discounts when you switch lenders. It can also help you by making it possible for you to restart your loan term because consolidated loans are generally considered to be new loans. It can reset the timeline on things like deferments and forbearances, and this can provide you with ample time to come up with a proper spending plan so that you are able to make all of your payments.

Dealing with Debt

Minimalist differs from a lot of other people when it comes to the way they deal with debt. First of all, minimalists don't believe in the idea that some forms of debt are technically good. There are economists who subscribe to the school of thought that it's a good thing to have some debt so that you can use your repayment history as proof of how reliable you are at making payments, in hopes to increase your chances of getting larger loans. Minimalists see the fatal flaw in that logic – the idea that you need to have debt to increase your chances of acquiring more debt (in the form of bigger loans) seems like a trap that is designed to keep you reliant on financial institutions so that they can squeeze as much interest out of you as possible.

Think about it for a second. You spend the whole month buying things with credit cards, most of which you can actually pay for out of pocket. At the end of the month, you pay that debt with interest, and you do the same with several other cards. If you make your payments on time, you get a good credit score. If your payments are late, that is reflected negatively in your credit score. Your credit score is shared with credit bureaus so that if you want a loan from a bank, they'll refer to that score to decide whether to give you a loan and what your interest rate for that loan is going to be. At the risk of sounding like a conspiracy theorist, I should point out that this looks like a system that is carefully designed to keep you indebted forever. They are so good at it to the point that they've convinced most people that debt is a good thing.

To minimalists, the idea of 'good debt' is a myth. The only difference between various kinds of debts is that some are bad while others are much worse. So, as a minimalist, your primary goal is to be debt-free. Minimalism is about freeing yourself from consumerism, and debt is the demon-child of consumerism. When you create your spending plan or budget, you should factor in a system that allows you to pay off all your debt as fast as possible. The fact is that you will never feel truly free unless you pay off all your debt. When you have a debt to pay, you feel like you are doing all the work and someone else is reaping all the rewards. There is no getting around paying your debt, so the best you can hope for is to get rid of the debt so that you can know what true freedom feels like.

Imagine having your paycheck come in, and you then get to keep all your cash because you don't have any debts to pay. You don't see chunks of your cash disappearing because you have to service a car loan, a student loan, a mortgage, and credit card payments. When you don't have those debts hanging over you, it will feel a bit strange at first—then, you will realize that you are feeling free for the first time in a long time.

If you are still young and you haven't accumulated a lot of debt, you might want to drop the bad habit of debt-financing all your major purchases. If you want to buy a car, instead of taking out a loan to pay for that car, you can get a cheap but functional car and use it for the time being, and then save your money until you have enough to get the car that you want. This method is going to be really difficult to implement because you have the urge to drive around in a nice car right now, but that urge is just a sign that your consumerist tendencies are trying to creep back up, so you need to learn to suppress those urges. You may not get to show off in a new car right now, but you also won't have to pay outrageous interest rates on a new car loan - that sounds more like showing off to me.

Paying off debts should be a bigger priority. There is no point of saving money when you have debts hanging over you. If you have savings that are more than your basic emergency fund (a basic emergency fund covers all your expenses for around three months), use that money to pay off your debt before you start saving again. Loans attract higher interest rates than the ones that you get from the best savings accounts, so if you save money while you still have debts, you will actually be making a net loss.

Automating All Your Bill Payments

Minimalism is about simplifying things, so when it comes to creating a minimalist spending plan, it's important to make it very easy for you to execute that plan. One way you can do that is by automating the bill payment process. There are a lot of people who skip paying their bills, not because they lack the cash to make payments, but because they lack time to sit down and handle their bills one by one. Paying your bills is probably the least enjoyable thing that you can do. You will be spending a lot of time filling out boring forms as you watch your money disappear into the hands of utility companies and creditors. This can be a rather stressful experience, especially if you are forgoing some of the things you enjoy doing just so you can afford to make those payments.

Automating your bill payment process makes the whole thing less painful, and it reduces the amount of time and effort that you have to put in when you make payments.

There are several methods that you can use to automate your bill payments. You can automate the process through your bank. In this case, all you would have to do is give your bank all the information about the bills that you need to pay every month, and then the bank would proceed to make all payments on your behalf. When your salary is reflected in your account, your bank will take out the payments for each bill and send them to the accounts of the companies to which you are making those payments.

Some banks also have online bill payment portals where you can log in and set automatic payments to a list of creditors. You would have to specify amounts that you need to send out to each creditor, and the bank will do it the same way that it moves cash from your checking account to your savings account and vice versa.

You can also automate your loan payment processes by giving creditors the authority to withdraw the amount that you owe them from your account and to pay it to themselves. In this method, you will have to provide each creditor with your banking information—then, the creditor will liaise with the bank so that they can take out the money directly from your account without violating your rights to privacy.

When you automate your bill payment process, you will be able to save a lot of time, which you can spend doing something less stressful and more rewarding. Automating your payments also makes it much easier for you to stick to your spending plan and to avoid the temptation of forgoing a bill payment so that you can spend the money on something that you consider to be fun.

As a point of caution, remember that when you automate your bill payments, you still have to make periodic checks to ensure that your bank or the creditor hasn't made an error that could cause complications. Even the best banks can sometimes make mistakes, so you have to crosscheck things to make sure that you don't lose your hard earned money.

Financial Planning

When you create a financial plan, you have to make sure that the plan incorporates all your goals, and it doesn't negate any of your values. We have already discussed how you can figure out what your goals are, so here, we will focus more on making sure that your financial plan adheres to your values.

A good financial plan should serve as a roadmap to help you figure out how you can find the necessary cash flow which you will use to bankroll your quest as you try to achieve each one of your goals. Unlike a spending plan, a financial plan is more than just how you spend the cash. It covers how you can get the cash, save it, invest it, and spend it. In financial planning, you concern yourself with how you spend each dollar you make, as well as what you can do to make more money.

In personal finance, a financial plan would include possible ideas as to how you can boost your income by making more money at work, or by starting a side hustle to supplement your income. However, when we look at financial planning from a minimalist perspective, we are more concerned with learning to live within our own means while spending our time doing work that we are passionate about. Minimalism doesn't encourage people to break their backs just so that they can make more money to accomplish goals that add no value to their lives. Instead, minimalism teaches people to be more contented with what they have and to make their income count more by avoiding wasting money on unnecessary material possessions.

If your goal was to save enough money to buy a nice car in a couple of years, a traditional personal finance expert might tell you to pick up a few extra shifts at work or to take a second job to be able to raise money within the stipulated time frame. However, a minimalist would ask you to recalibrate your goal, so that instead of saving up to buy a fancy car, you will be more realistic about the amount of cash that you can raise within that period, then find a more affordable car model within your price range which you can then purchase when the time comes.

Financial planning also involves selecting various investments so that you can grow your savings and be able to live more comfortably when you are retired. If you want to invest according to your values as a minimalist, you should try to keep things as simple as possible by just investing your money in ETFs (exchange-traded funds). These funds may have small returns, but they are generally safer, and they don't take up too much of your time. You can just invest, set the investment aside, and then focus on things you are passionate about and let the funds grow.

creating a spending plan

There are many different ways that you can go about creating a minimalist spending plan. Some methods are simple while others can be quite complicated, but the thing to remember is that there are no hard and fast rules as to how you need to format your budget, so you can look at all the methods out there and come up with one that works well for you.

A spending plan is defined as a statement or an action plan that you can use to coordinate the way that you intend to utilize your resources towards taking care of certain expenditures. It's a detailed plan that outlines the rules you plan on following when it comes to the way you spend your money, and the way you deal with many other money-related issues. It's a sort of agreement or resolution that you come up with to help you track your own finances so that you don't end up spending too much where you shouldn't, or too little in areas that should be a priority.

One of the most common methods that people use when they are creating their spending plans is the "balanced money formula" method. This method is quite simple. It suggests that you spend 50% of your income on the things that you need, 20% on your savings, and 30% on the things that you want. This method is very simple because it makes it possible for you to assess what you can afford to have to depend on the income that you generate, so you never have to live beyond your means.

The things that you need include the basics that you can't live without, such as your house payments, your utility bills, your essential clothing, your gas money, and of course, your groceries. The things that you want include your nonessential clothing items, your new high-end electronics, tickets to games and concerts, snacks, your cable TV subscriptions, and many other things that you would still be able to survive if you didn't have. The percentage that goes into your savings can also be used to pay off debts.

While the balanced money formula is great in general, it somehow negates the principles of minimalism because it allocates such a big chunk of your disposable income to pay for the things that you want but could do without. In keeping with the rules of minimalism, if you want to use this formula, you can try to modify it a little bit so that you reduce the percentage of income that goes into paying for your wants, and increase the percentage that goes into your savings. Minimalists should avoid using this method before they modify it, because the way it is right now, it makes it quite easy for one to overspend. That being said, this formula is great for minimalists because it simplifies all expenses by putting them into three general categories so that you can have an easier time deciding the priority level of each of them.

Another way of creating a spending plan is by using the envelop method, which is also known as the cash-only method. In this method, you assess your past spending behavior and determine how much money you need for each particular spending category for the duration of the month. You then make a withdrawal of the amount of cash that you need for all the categories and then put the cash for each category in a different envelope. If you decide that you will spend $500 on groceries, you will put that amount of money in an envelope, label it accordingly, and use it as your only source of money when you purchase groceries.

The point is that irrespective of what you want to buy at any given day in that month, the important thing is that the amount should be adequate for all your grocery expenses until the next month comes around and you have a new envelope. This method is great for people who tend to overspend on impulse purchases, and it can be effective in making you think twice before you buy something you don't need, because you will always be trying to spend less so that you don't exceed your limit. The main issue with this method is the risk involved in keeping large sums of money around at all times. If you can figure out a way to keep your money safe, you are okay to try this method because it is in line with most of the principles of minimalism.

There is also the 'zero-based' method of creating a spending plan. In this method, you have to assign a particular function to each and every dollar, so that you don't have any money that is idle in any way. Each dollar that gets into your account goes out to do something very specific. When we say that you assign a function to each dollar, it doesn't mean that you spend it, it just means that you give it a purpose. For instance, when your money goes into your retirement or your savings account, then that is the purpose that it is serving.

Each dollar you make will be given a specific job, whether it is to cover your utility bill, to pay off your loan, or to cover your mortgage. This method is great for minimalists because it gives us absolute control over our finances so that we don't have to spend a single dollar without planning for it. The downside of this type of spending plan is that it can be quite time consuming because it requires you to figure out what each dollar should go into, and it requires a lot of record keeping. Because the execution of this method is quite involving, there is a high likelihood that the people who use it could burn out and decide to abandon their spending plans altogether.

Another method of creating a spending plan is known as "the 60% solution." In this method, 60% of all your income is used for something called "committed expenses." The person who created this method refers to "committed expenses" as things like your groceries, car and mortgage payments, insurance, bills, and other things for which paying is an obligation. In this method, all expenses that are essentially commitments are considered to be essential, which means that things like your phone and internet bills are thought of as needs, and not wants. When you are done with the 60%, the remaining 40% is split into 4 similar amounts (10% each), and each amount goes into one of 4 things. Those things include your retirement fund, your, long term savings, your short term savings, and your "fun money." In this method, it is recommended that the amounts that go into the retirement fund, the long term savings, and the short term savings, should be automated so that you never really get to touch any of that money.

This type of spending plan is recommended for people who like to automate things, which means that it could be useful

to minimalists. However, the problem with this budget method is that if you make a lot of money, it makes it easy for you to overspend. As a minimalist, if you find that you make a lot more money so that you can cover most of your expenses with less than 60% of your income, you can tweak this budget a little bit so that you increase your savings and you spend less. If you make little money, this budget is perfect for you because it essentially forces you to live within your means
in addition to saving money
.   You can also create a values-based spending plan. This plan is particularly popular with young adults who are in the medium to the high-income category. The way it works is that you apply your values to how you spend your money. When coming up with a spending plan using this method, you have to write down your values and then only spend money on things that align with those values. The problem with this method is that it doesn't specify whether you should prioritize constructive values, or whether you should shun out negative values. For example, if one of your values is that you like people to perceive you as rich, this method would allow you to make purchase decisions in service of that value. If you are a minimalist, you can use this method and combine it with minimalistic values, so that you have a values-based minimalist spending plan.

Now that we have discussed various common methods of creating a spending plan, I recommend that you use those methods only as templates and that you take the time to create your own unique spending plan. You can borrow the good ideas from the methods that we have discussed, but you should leave out the ideas that don't suit your particular situation or those that negate your values. The best spending plan for you would probably be a combination of 2 or more methods mentioned above. In the end, no one can tell you which spending plan method will work for you and which one won't. You need to consider your specific needs, and you need to look inward and be honest with yourself about what you can manage and what you can't. If you know that you are easily tempted to make extravagant purchases, you can't come up with a spending plan that uses a hands-off approach. If you know that you won't have time to monitor your expenses closely, you can't come up with a plan that requires a lot of your personal time. Create your spending plan however you like, but the important thing is that you should make it very clear so that there is no ambiguity about what you can and can't do, and you should do everything in your power to stick to that plan.

Getting Used to Feeling Different from the New Spending Plan

When you create a spending plan and start to execute it, you have to remember that you are completely overhauling a financial system that you have been using for years, which means that things are going to feel completely different. One of the main reasons why people fail to follow through with their well thought out spending plans is that they are often unable to get over the initial shock that comes with the drastic changes that they make, and they resort back to a trend that they are more comfortable with.

You need to be mentally prepared for things to get tough and uncomfortable. When you are used to expensive snacks, you will find the healthier more affordable ones horrible at first, but you have to keep your end goal in mind. You are going to feel a little off if you decide to give up buying expensive coffee every morning, but you have to remind yourself that what you are doing is a lot more important, and you are benefitting your future self in the process.

One way to motivate yourself to stick to your spending plan is by making sure that you make one of your earlier goals a 'reward goal.' When you create a spending plan, most of the money you will be saving will be going towards things like your retirement, your savings account, your emergency fund, and even debt repayment. This can feel depressing because you won't be seeing any short term results of your efforts. That is why it's recommended that when you get started, and when you create your goals, you should make one of your short term goals something rewarding so that you can stay motivated to stick to your spending plan.

For example, if there is something useful that you have always wanted to buy, but you never got around to it (a good example would be a small desk for a corner in your living room that you want to turn into a home office), make it a short term financial goal, and save for it for the first couple of months that you are on your new spending plan. When you have enough money, and you buy it, that will serve as a proof of concept that your plan really works, and it can motivate you to keep saving your cash towards some of your medium and long-term goals.

Putting the Spending Plan into Practice

A well thought out spending plan means nothing without action. This is going to be the most challenging and difficult part of the whole process. It's easy to be idealistic and to tell yourself in a logical manner that you are going to cut your expenses here and there, but the execution of that plan, is where the real work is. Supposing, for example, you notice that you spend $100 a month on Starbucks coffee, and you, with all the optimism in the world, decide that you are going to eliminate that expense from your life altogether, and use that money to help chip away at your debt payments each month. It's easy to reset that expense to zero on paper and to allocate that money to something else, but the execution is going to be a lot more difficult.

Sticking to a spending plan is about finding the motivation to carry on with it despite the difficulty and the temptation. Motivation is a tricky thing, but when you learn how to find it, it can help you overcome some of life's most difficult challenges.

One way to ensure that you stick to your spending plan is to find the main reason why you chose to create that spending plan in the first place, and then remind yourself of it every time the going gets tough. Even if you have similar motivations, values, and principles, the underlying reason why someone starts a spending plan is never the same — it varies from person to person, and it's informed by personal experience. You may be trying to be more responsible with your cash so that you can be a good role model for your kids. You may be doing it in order to save your marriage, which has been strained by financial problems. You may be doing it so that you can afford to retire by 40. Whatever core reason drove you to create the spending plan in the first place—you should hold on to it, and you must never lose sight of it.

If you make a specific spending change in your life, you have to find a way to offset that change because the spending behavior that you are trying to eliminate is still a desire that you have, and unless you can fill it with something else, your chances of relapsing are going to be pretty high. In the example where you have to reduce the amount of money that you spend on coffee each month and redirect it to your debt payments, you can offset that change or make it more manageable by making your coffee at home each morning. You are still getting that much-needed dose of caffeine that your body craves, without spending an unnecessary amount of money on it each month.

Another way to ensure that you stick to your minimalist spending plan is to make yourself accountable to the public. You may be able to share your spending plan online (e.g., on social media or on a personal blog) and keep your followers, your friends, and your family members updated on how well you are doing with the plan. When you are tempted to spend money on something that negates your plan, you will feel motivated to overcome that temptation because you know that the people in your life are rooting for you and your plan. When we are accountable to other people, we tend to step up our efforts to carry on with difficult things because we don't want to be publicly perceived as failures. There are also a lot of forums online where minimalists exchange ideas and share their personal experiences on how they save money and how they manage to live on less, so you can join some of those forums to find the motivation to carry on with your plan. More importantly, you may find the motivation to carry on with your plan when you share it with the most important people in your life.

Another way to be able to stick to your spending plan as a minimalist is to use a visualization board. Being a minimalist doesn't mean that you don't have any dreams of your own. You still have lots of dreams, including owning a reasonably sized home, a reasonably priced car, and having enough savings to give you the freedom that you need to live a comfortable and happy life as you get older. You can create a vision board of your own to encourage yourself to stay focused on your goal. You can create a physical board, or a digital one, as long as it has pictorial representations of your dreams so that it can serve to remind you about them. However, you need to be careful when using a vision board as a minimalist because it's easy to fall back into the trap of consumerism if you spend a lot of time looking at photos of material possessions.

You need to reward yourself from time to time in order to stay motivated to stick with your spending plan. If your spending plan is too strict and it doesn't allow room for any kind of fun, you are going to feel as though you are punishing yourself, and this increases your chances of waking up one day and deciding to give up on the plan altogether. You have to remember to set aside some money to treat yourself once in a while, but you have to make sure that your little indulgence doesn't contradict the values and goals you set for yourself in the first place. You can choose to travel to a place you have never been to before, to go see some attractions, etc. As a minimalist, remember that experiences are more valuable than physical possessions, so make sure that you do something that will add value to your life, and something that you will remember for a long time.

As you execute your spending plan, you have to remember that this is a whole new lifestyle that you have chosen to lead, so stop looking back at your old system and stop thinking that you can always return to it. Understand that this is a forward journey and that for you, looking back is not an option. This is how you do things now, and it is how things are going to be for the rest of your life.

the psychology of habit formation

As you implement your spending plan, you want to make sure that you concentrate on turning it into a habit, because when something becomes a habit, it essentially becomes second nature, meaning you do it naturally without giving it much thought. Scientists believe that there are three basic stages that are involved in the formation of a habit, and the habit in question is formed if these stages are repeated many times in a continuous loop. The 3 stages are the Cue, the Routine and the Reward. To put it in the simplest terms possible, when our brains identify a cue, act on that cue in a certain way, and receive a certain reward, they become wired to repeat that same process in the future. Because of the way the habit loop works, and the way that our environments are filled with stimuli that encourage consumerism, it is very easy for you to form a negative spending habit, and it's quite difficult for you to form a positive one.

For example, if you are sitting on a couch watching the TV and you see a pizza commercial, that is a cue. Your response can be to call the pizza place and place an order. The reward is the great tasting pizza that you will be eating within the hour. A few days later, when that commercial comes on again, you may find yourself going through the same process, and with time, you might not even notice it, but a bad habit has been formed. Bad spending habits are easy to form because the cues are so enticing, and the rewards come almost immediately after the response, but that doesn't mean you can't break those bad habits and develop good ones instead.

The thing to remember about habits is that you can't forget bad habits, but you can be able to modify the habit loops in your brain and change bad habits into good ones. You do this by trying to ignore cues, altering your response to certain cues, or delaying/eliminating the chances of getting a reward. Suppose you are trying to stick to a budget, but you tend to be a compulsive shopper. Every time you see a picture of something nice on a magazine, a catalog, or online, you are tempted to make a purchase. In this case, you should reduce the chances of coming across a cue by trying to stop reading magazines. You can also try to change your response to the cue by making it hard for you to get your hands on a credit card in order to go shopping. Since your reward will be delayed, the gratification won't be as strong, and this can help you attach less importance to that particular negative habit loop.

You can also form good spending habits using your knowledge of habit loops. In most cases, it works best when you change the way you respond to a cue. That means that when you encounter a cue, you have to change the routine that you follow so that it doesn't lead you to a negative result. When that same pizza commercial comes on as you are watching the TV, and you feel the urge to pick up your phone and place an order, make a conscious effort to walk over to the fridge, take out a handful of baby carrots, and start munching on them. Do this over and over again every time you see the same commercial until it becomes a habit. That way, you will end up changing the bad habit of ordering pizza, and you will manage to develop a good habit of eating a healthy snack instead.

It's a Process, Not an Event

Using a spending plan can be transformational, and like any major change in your life, it's going to come with a lot of bumps. You won't be perfect when you start implementing your plan, but then again, nobody is ever really perfect. You have to make sure that you stay committed and dedicated as you put your plan into practice because your financial and your personal freedom depend on your ability to stick with your plan and to see it through. Even if you experience considerable setbacks, don't ever give up. You should recalibrate your expectations, and keep trying to work towards implementing your spending plan and attaining your financial freedom.

Apply Periodic Spending Plan Checks

Finally, to be able to succeed at sticking to your spending plan, you have to make sure that you keep track of your successes, and that you cherish all the small victories and milestones that you pass along the way. You should apply periodic checks to see if you are sticking to your spending plan, and you should monitor your milestones to see if you are meeting all of them. I suggest checking in weekly and updating all of your income/expenses at the end of each week. This helps you to stay on top of the money coming in and the money going out. If you notice that you have deviated significantly from your budget, you can review all areas where you notice missteps, and you can come up with new strategies to make sure that you keep on complying with the requirements of your budget.

Supposing you are trying to save $10,000 over a number of years. This number may feel high, and you may feel overwhelmed by it, but you can stay motivated if you take a moment to pat yourself on the back with each milestone that you cross, however small it may be. For every 10 dollars, you save, think of it as a step that you have taken in a journey of 1000 steps. When you hit the $100, $500, and $1000 markers, you can share the news with the people that are close to you, and you can find a small way to celebrate your achievement, however small it may seem. When you celebrate each small milestone, in essence, what you are doing is breaking a giant challenge into small chunks, and this makes it so much easier for you to take the next step and the one after that.

The "Living with Less" Lifestyle

When you are content with what you have, and when you don't owe anything to anyone, you live a life that is generally free of stress and anxiety, resulting in much greater happiness. If you are a consumerist and you have a lot of debt, you may live in a nice, large and expensive house, but it's always going to feel as though the wolves are at your door. It always feels that if you skip a single day of the rat race, you are going to fall behind, and the financial institutions are going to kick your door down and take your "valuable" possessions away. With consumerism, you are never content, and your mind is never at peace. The minimalist spending plan is intended to help you put an end to all that.

Although people keep telling you that debt is a tool that can help you grow and that repayments can serve as motivators to keep you working, the truth is that as humans, we are at our best when we aren't under someone else's thumb. That is what being debt free and stress-free does for you — it allows you to be the best version of yourself. It gives you the freedom to do the things that you are passionate about. It makes it possible for you to spend more time nurturing your children, your relationships, your passions and your positive habits.

When you learn to live with less, you find intrinsic reasons to be happy, and you discover real and lasting happiness. You learn to be confident, not because you gain the admiration of others, but because you learn to respect yourself. You know deep within that you are among the few people that have the courage to live within their own means, and you understand that confidence is not something that is bought, but it's something that is found freely in all of us. You learn to hold yourself to your own standards and values, instead of losing your own identity trying to meet standards that society sets for you. You drive around in a budget friendly car with a proud smile on your face knowing you aren't forfeiting a sizable chunk of your paycheck to a dealership every month.

You understand that your lifestyle requires you to make a lot of sacrifices and to forgo a lot of your material desires—but these sacrifices lead to a much more fulfilling life. Most importantly, you are free from regrets. You are free from the regret of paying too much for a car or breaking your back to make mortgage payments instead of making the decision to spend more time with your loved ones. I'm not going to lie and tell you that it will be a blissful experience all the time, but I can tell you that it's going to be the most satisfying and rewarding thing you have ever done.

Conclusion

The next step is to apply the techniques that you have learned here to craft your own unique and detailed spending plan as you keep the principles of minimalism in mind.

There are five basic principles of minimalism that will come in handy as you try to get better at implementing your financial planning and at managing your expenses. The first principle that applies here is the one about eliminating needless things. In general, this principle applies in areas such as decluttering and organization, but it's still very relevant when it comes to creating a spending plan. You need to omit the expenses that you don't need, the accounts that are duplicated unnecessarily, and the credit cards that you could very well do without. It's after you have gotten rid of the clutter in your financial dealings that you will be able to see clearly what you have and what your true wealth potential is.

The second principle that you need to remember to apply as you create a spending plan is the principle that talks about identifying the essential things in your life. In order for you to live comfortably with what you have and to focus your financial resources in areas where they can have the most positive impact on your life, you first have to identify what those essential areas are. You cannot be successful if you don't *define* success correctly. By helping you identify the essentials, minimalism makes it possible for you to have the right spending goals.

The third principle of minimalism that applies here is the principle of making everything count. This principle teaches you that every dollar is important; that as you create your spending plan, you should make sure that no single dollar goes to waste; and that all money does is help you work towards achieving your goals. This principle also teaches you to make all of your time count, as many people assume that they are still too young to start using a spending plan to make better financial decisions.

The fourth principle of minimalism that applies to personal finance is the one that teaches you to do things that fill your life with joy. When you apply this principle to your spending plan, it helps you to manage your money in a way that allows you the freedom to stop chasing money you don't have, but rather saving it or putting it towards life experiences for you and your loved ones. If you spend all your money as soon as it comes in instead of using it wisely, you will never have the freedom and the peace of mind that you need to truly live a life of joy.

The final principle of minimalism that applies here is the principle of constant self-improvement. Minimalism is never a done deal. It's a journey that you are on, and it's an idea that you keep striving towards. When you create your spending plan and try to implement it, you will hit some bumps in the road—life happens. Minimalists aren't perfect, but they don't stop working towards perfecting their dedication to living more fulfilling lives by learning to live with less. As you implement your spending plan, don't expect to be perfect at doing it—just keep trying to make yourself better.

If you learn the principles of minimalism and take them to heart, they will help you to achieve financial freedom in several ways. These principles teach you everything you need to know in order to figure out the correct way of prioritizing your spending. Most other approaches to financial planning don't focus any attention on your personal values, and they can easily guide you down the wrong path so that you work hard and save your money only to spend it on something that you don't need. Minimalism teaches you to identify what you need and don't need in the first place.

Minimalism teaches you that you need less space—thus helping you save on your rent or your mortgage. As a minimalist, you aren't hoarding things—so even when you live in a small space, it will feel spacious and comfortable. You can even sell off some of your unnecessary possessions and raise a significant amount of money, which you can then direct towards paying down your debts.

Minimalism enables you to stay laser-focused when it comes to achieving your financial goals and staying within the limits of your spending plan. If you haven't yet embraced minimalism and are trying to cut down on certain expenditures, you have to go up against a cognitive dissonance in your head, as your mind may be wired to think that certain materialistic things are "good" for you and that eliminating them is "bad." However, as a minimalist, you believe in the principle that materialistic things are bad, so when you decide to cut yourself off, your whole brain will be on the same page—hence, psychologically speaking, you have a better chance of succeeding at it.

You spent your valuable time reading through this book because deep within, you really want to improve your financial situation. You want to be a more responsible spender, and you want to break the chains of consumerism. In the book, I tried as much as possible to explain how you can use a combination of spending plans and the principles of minimalism to turn yourself into the responsible spender that you have always wanted to be. The ball is in your court now, and it's up to you to apply this knowledge to the best of your ability in order to regain control of your finances.

No matter how bad the situation has gotten, you can always turn things around when you learn to change your mindset and to return to the basics. Consumerism and materialism deny you your freedom. At the end of the day, it's better to live under the humblest of circumstances than it is to live in a house of cards for which you have to labor and toil your whole life. I am not asking you to cut yourself off from society and to go live off the grid—I am merely telling you that as much as you want to be a part of society, don't let it dictate what you should own and spend your hard-earned money on.

You have seen in this book how deeply the lie of consumerism runs, so as a minimalist, the best service that you can do for the people you care about is to show them that they, too, can earn back their freedom by creating and implementing minimalist spending plans of their own. When you work hard at regaining control of your financial situation, you will start succeeding—and the people around you are going to notice that even though you are humbler and more down-to-earth, you seem happier and more fulfilled. They will start asking questions because they, too, are dissatisfied with the constant agony of working for material possessions. When this happens, don't be selfish, and don't be secretive. Share your story with them, communicate to them the principles that you have learned, and tell them about your journey. When the opportunity arises, be a force for good and help others around you to regain their financial freedom as well.

As you start your first step on the journey towards financial minimalism, make sure that you take pictures along the way—one day, you will look back, and you will be amazed at what you have accomplished just by changing the way you think about material things and by trying the best that you can to live with less. You will learn along the way to find joy in simple things, and you will develop a spirit that is more generous than you ever imagined.